The Price and the Prize

THE Price AND THE Prize

Culbert G. Rutenber

BROADMAN PRESS
Nashville, Tennessee

Revised Edition

© Copyright 1953, 1981 • Broadman Press

All rights reserved.

4262-30

ISBN: 0-8054-6230-9

Dewey Decimal Classification: 234

Subject heading: SALVATION

Library of Congress Catalog Card Number: 81-65392

Printed in the United States of America

To one who shall, indeed, be named
because the beauty of her name
is symbolic of the beauty
of her spirit
To Duron

Introduction

This book has a history. It began with a series of articles in a Youth magazine. Amended and enlarged, it graduated to the status of a book. Now, after several printings, it is undergoing its first revision. Given a face-lifting and outfitted with appropriate cosmetic touches, this revised version moves onto the stage to make its contribution to the evangelization of our youth. This at least is the hope and prayer of the author.

Times change and customs, too, but the Word of our God endures forever. It would be laughable nonsense to claim that this small volume is the Word of God. But it is neither laughable nor nonsense to say that it is as faithful an effort to interpret that Word, as given in the gospel, as the limitations of space and the understanding of the author permit.

I thank Howard Bramlette, editor of *The Baptist Student,* for shepherding this revised edition from my hands to those of the publisher.

CULBERT G. RUTENBER

Austin, Texas
1981

Contents

1. Where Misery Abounds...........11

2. The Trouble with Us Is...........21

3. God Steps onto the Stage.........31

4. Redemption from Guilt...........41

5. Redemption from Perversion......49

6. Redemption from Lovelessness....59

7. Redemption to Goodness........69

8. The Conquering Christ...........75

9. The Price and the Prize...........89

1
Where Misery Abounds

Humpty Dumpty sat on a wall.
Humpty Dumpty had a great fall.
And all the king's horses and all the king's men
Couldn't put Humpty Dumpty together again.

We live in a Humpty Dumpty civilization. Our world has had a great fall, and all the learned experts and all the wise men have failed to find the glue to stick it together again. It may be that we live in "one world," but it is "one" only in its pains and afflictions.

"Gospels of redemption" inevitably arise in such a world. It has not been terribly long ago that we fought a war to keep from being "redeemed" by one of them—Fascism. Though that particular form of Fascism was defeated, the movement is still around and surfaces from time to time in one country or another. In more recent times, the world has been confronted with "redemption" from another quarter—Communism. It begins to look as though a major task of ours will have to be working and praying to be saved from these spurious kinds of "salvation."

Fascism and Communism are gospels of redemption by force. Democracy, on the other hand, is not a power unto salvation at all, although it frequently is offered as such, indeed, as the only alternative to the secular religions mentioned above. Democracy is an opportunity—nothing more (though that is much). It stresses freedom but is dumb to the larger question, freedom for what? It preserves liberties but does not in itself inform a people as to what to do with them. That is why democracy is both hard to transplant and easy to lose, where misery abounds.

There is, of course, still another gospel of redemption. It does not offer salvation by a club but salvation by a cross. This is harder and less immediately attractive to those who, in their impatience, would like to save the world in the next twenty-four hours: push-button redemption by an ill-yoked crew of blundering idealists and ruthless opportunists. From such dangerous deliveries we would gladly be delivered. True deliverance is neither simple ("just eliminate private ownership of the means of production") nor easily achieved. It has a high price tag. Yet, strangely, the high cost of deliverance—blood and pain and suffering—is not primarily ours to pay at all, but God's. Or, better, it is first God's and then ours as we share the passion of One who became the partner of our destiny that we may become the heirs of his. Christianity deals with salvation by the cross of God.

Christianity may be true or it may be false. It may be good or it may be bad. It may make sense or it may make nonsense. But before any judgment can be made upon it, it must first be understood. And, oddly enough, though it has been ignored, hated, rejected, feared, attacked, it just as frequently has been misunderstood. Many thinkers believe that the twentieth century has had a harder time understanding what the Christian gospel is all about than any previous century! The twentieth century has remade the gospel of God into its own image and likeness and in the remaking has altered it beyond recognition. It thought to "touch up" the face of Christ by a little plastic surgery but succeeded only in making him unrecognizable.

The type of "Christianity" which has been most popular during the twentieth century is called by Theodore Wedel the log-cabin-to-White-House approach.[1] It is a good label, for America has dearly loved the Abraham-Lincoln-type of story. According to this kind of approach, Jesus Christ is a bigger, better, and wiser Abraham Lincoln. He started out in a manger, but he ended up on a throne. He began as a peasant, but he became the king of human hearts. He commenced as a simple, itinerant preacher, but he lived so beautifully and taught so divinely that he has been well called the Son of God. He so identified himself with his Heavenly Father and his purposes that he could say, "I and my Father are one" (John 10:30). God was in him more than in any other man; he revealed what God is like. He calls us to follow him, to live as he lived, and to obey his teachings. If we follow in his footsteps, we too may proceed from the log cabin of our lower selves to the White House in the sky and dwell with God forever more.

The log-cabin-toWhite-House approach might be called a religion of "in order that." One holds high ideals, serves his fellowman, and follows Christ *in order that* he may be saved and go to heaven. God serves a double function in this scheme. First, he gives friendly encouragement and help to the pilgrim who is trying to do his best. And secondly, God keeps the score during the pilgrimage, adding up the failures and successes in separate columns, balancing one column against the other, and thus determining the pilgrim's final rating. This is the justice of God. But since God is also merciful, he does not keep a very accurate account of the failures. Indeed, he sometimes overlooks failures completely (as though he had not seen them), and at other times he excuses them because he realizes that the pilgrim really could not help it, it was not his fault. God understands as well as the next fellow that we all are human, after all. This aspect of God's dealings with men is called the love of God. In an in-order-that religion, God is important, but the real hero is the man who rises to the challenge, adopts the ideals of Christ as his own, and sticks to them through thick and thin.

Now a log-cabin-to-White-House approach may be very understandable, very simple, and very appealing. But Canon Wedel is quite correct when he says that it must not be confused with Christianity. Christianity is just the opposite. Christianity is, in Wedel's words, a White-House-to-long-cabin story. Humans were so earthbound in the mud of their own making that they could not even "get off the ground" to soar into the stratosphere where high ideals reign. Or to change the figure, they were so mired in the quicksand of their own follies that they could not even get their feet on the highway to the city of God, let alone walk it. The quicksand meant death. But God would not leave people to this fate. The desperate plight of people pulled the All-Loving

One off his throne and sent him hastening to the dark and dangerous wilderness of blasted hopes, to rescue people as only God can.

We called the log-cabin-to-White-House approach an in-order-that religion. We might call the White-House-to-log-cabin approach a because-of religion. "We love him, because he first loved us" (1 John 4:19). The hero of the story is not good-living man, but all-loving God. The blood, the sweat, the tears were his, and to him belong the praise and thanks. People who have been rescued by God are so grateful that they are impelled to love God and do his will in the service of fellow human being. Because God has done so much for us, we must do all we can for God.

A friend of mine once saw a man rescue a boy from drowning in Arrowhead Lake, California. The boy was so far gone that artificial respiration had to be administered by his rescuer. On regaining consciousness, the boy's gratitude was intense. "Thank you so much," he breathed, "for saving my life."

"Think nothing of it," smiled his redeemer. "Let us now see to it that the life saved was worth the saving."

But it is time we got down to the real business at hand—taking a sharp look at the Christian faith and its claim to be a gospel of redemption. Quicksand and highways and drowning and the White House are all very well, but they are picture terms and not the real thing. What *really* is our trouble and what has God *really* done about it? If we raise *those* questions, we must begin by investigating the Christian meaning of a little three-letter word, *sin*. For if we don't understand that, none of the rest will make any sense.

Note

1. Canon Theodore Wedel, *The Christianity of Main Street,* Copyright 1950 by The Macmillan Company.

2
The
Trouble with
Us Is . . .

Stanley High, at the time an editor of the *Reader's Digest* and a nationally-known speaker, gave an address a few years ago at Northfield, Massachusets. He made the following comments:

"I don't make any apology for putting the failure of the church on a personal level . . . I think that the first business of the church is to redeem me. And I don't mean to redeem me in the purely social sense which convinces me that the Golden Rule ought to be my Confession of Faith. By redeeming me, I mean personal redemption—the process by which I'm spiritually shaken apart and spiritually put together again, and from which I—the personal I—emerge a totally different person. . . .

"The first reason for this failure is that the church . . . rates me altogether too highly. . . . I'm simply not as good as modern Protestantism assumes me to be. . . . It has assumed that all I needed was the right hand of fellowship, when . . . what I am in greater need of is a kick in the pants."

That is a highly interesting passage. A man's view of human nature is the basis of his thinking. The reason is obvious: One's interpretation of human nature determines one's idea of God and of salvation. If humans are not so bad, then salvation is not so important. If humans are radically evil, then only a radical cure can save them.

At times Christians have taken a rather optimistic view of human nature; but for the most part, the exact opposite has been true. The Christian faith takes a dim view of humanity. It has a blunt label for people—sinners. And the sin which it sees people in is not something accidental, partial, secondary. People are sinners at their very center. This description does not mean our situation is hopeless, for we have possibilities of good that redemption can make real. But until we are redeemed by Christ, we are evil—radically evil.

This dose is too strong for some people. They would not deny that people can go wrong, terribly wrong; but they want to add that we can also go right, gloriously right. There is something of good in everyone, they tell us. After all, are we not children of God, created in God's image?

Such a view needs examination, for while it involves a misunderstanding, it is not wholly false. Its error lies in failing to distinguish between humans as they were created and humans as they actually are. Let's listen to Stanley High again. Says he: "Ever since my Sunday school days, it has been dinned into me that I'm made in God's image. It seems to me that those who lay so much emphasis on my bearing such a resemblance to the Almighty are not only mistaken about me, they're also mistaken about history.

"Man was made in the image of God in the first chapter of Genesis. Then he had what the theologians call a Fall. He's never been the same since—not on his own. . . . The whole of the Bible and the whole of the ministry of Jesus, as I understand it, were designated not to persuade man how good he is on his own, but how evil he is on his own. And how good, by process of redemption . . . he can become."[2]

That statement is exactly right. Sin is a corruption and perversion of an original goodness.

To speak of sin as a perversion is to admit that there was something worthwhile that got perverted. Sin is a parasite; it destroys. What it destroys is health, purity, and right functioning. Sin is like the rust which corrodes and makes tools useless. It is the good metal that is corroded and damaged by the rust. Or perhaps a poisoned glass of water would be a better illustration. There is nothing wrong with the water as mere H_2O, but there is something wholly wrong with the water which has been poisoned and corrupted by a lethal mixture. Nothing remains unaffected. Every particle of water is unfit for consumption, for every bit is tainted with the same poison.

Humans, then, are sinners. Their sinfulness is the first of all facts upon which the Christian system is built. But to make this statement mean something definite, we must inquire as to just what establishes humans' sinfulness. Is it because of the things they do? Only superficially. The things that are done are sins and we are investigating sin. The sins stem from the sin, and sin is a condition of life before it is an activity.

What, then, is sin itself? The best answer is given by one of the ancient prophets, "All we like sheep have gone astray; we have turned every one to his own way" (Isa. 53:6). There it is. Sin is having or wanting to have your own way. Just that! Such terrible sins as thievery or murder may not be involved at all. A person can be very ethical and highly moral, but still be as thoroughly self-centered as other people who express their selfishness in criminal ways.

Any effort of a person to guide and direct his own life sets that person up as a sinner, subject to the divine judgment. Sin is just wanting your own way and even a child can be and is a sinner!

Perhaps a word of caution should be injected here. The opposite of sin is not the virtue of laziness, or do-nothingism, or inertia and indifference. The Christian faith awards no prizes to drifters. The great Christians of all ages have been energetic workers. But their energy has been God-directed rather than self-directed. That's the point, and a big point it is. The whole tension between God and a person centers at this point: Who is going to be boss?

Sin, then, is humanity's effort to play God. People want their own ways when they should want God's way. People make themselves the centers of their lives (even of morally good lives), whereas God should be the center of life. When the Christian faith says people are sinners, it is aiming a blow at self-sufficiency. Self-sufficiency always implies pride; and pride perhaps is the greatest sin. In order to justify ourselves, we rehearse our virtues and form our pride upon them. But pride remains pride even when it concerns virtue (self-righteousness)—which is another way of saying that as long as "I" is at the center of life, neither our virtue nor our religious beliefs and practices can save us. The possibility of escaping from the humiliating label of "sinner" can arise only if we come to the end of ourselves and our self-sufficiency and let God take over.

If this explanation is what the Christian faith means by sin, then it is not very hard to believe that everybody is a sinner! We might even call in a witness, a consulting psychologist. Dr. Lawrence Gould says, "The normal development of a human personality is from uninhibited self-indulgence (since babies are born completely selfish) to socialization." So all people are born sinners![3] And if we do not want to take a psychologist's word for it, all we need to do is look around at our present tragic dilemma and at our past history. Something is pretty wrong somewhere. We like to talk of progress, but we might remember that progress does not extend to the basic traits of human nature. Professor Hooton, Harvard anthropologist of yesteryear was accustomed to stressing the fact that human nature has not changed since the Old Stone Age. Harry Emerson Fosdick once said that we may have improved upon the sickle of Ruth, the Old Testament heroine, but we have not improved upon Ruth.

Sin, then, is our trouble. We were made to live one way, and we are living just the opposite. We were not satisfied to stay put the way we were created. We had to run off and set up housekeeping for ourselves. We are in revolt against God, against our better selves, and against our fellow humans. In relation to God, our sin is guilt. In relation to ourselves, it is perversion. In relation to others, it is unbrotherliness and conflict. This spells tragedy all the way around—tragedy to God, tragedy to ourselves, and tragedy to our society.

An old Greek dramatist once suggested to his fellow craftsmen that a god should not be introduced upon the stage unless the situation was so serious as absolutely to demand it. If the Christian view of humanity is true, if the mess that sin has made is as tragic and hopeless as the Bible (and human history) indicates, then nothing less than God stepping onto the stage in a mighty act of redemption can clean up the mess and make things right.

Notes

1. Reprinted by permission from TIME, The Weekly Newsmagazine, Copyright Time Inc. 1947.
2. Ibid.

3. Sinners, but not guilty sinners. A baby is born with the natural tendency to make itself the center of the universe and in this sense is a sinner. But guilt does not arise until the growing child ratifies the selfish drive of its nature by giving conscious expression to it.

3
God Steps onto the Stage

When God set out to rescue humanity from the sinful mess into which it had fallen, he did not stand on the remote shore of heaven's majestic holiness and pluck at us with delicate fingers. He waded right into the middle of the muddle. This is the meaning of the coming of Jesus Christ. Not that God had been idle before he came to us in Jesus Christ. Far from it. But there came a time when God addressed himself to the very core of our human predicament. And this brought him into our human story in a new and decisive way.

Jesus Christ revealed to us fully the nature of God. Revelation sounds like a very mysterious and somewhat suspicious thing. But actually, in principle, it is quite an everyday occurrence. Revelation is merely the way persons make themselves known to each other. We do not come to know each other by staring and guessing or by putting sections of each other's body under the microscope. At best, this might bring us some little knowledge *about* each other. But when we actually come to *know* another, we do so because the other permits us to. He talks to us face to face and lives and does things before our very eyes. And by the things he says and the way he behaves, he reveals himself to us.

Since God is personal, he too must reveal himself to men in the things he says and the way he acts. But he must talk our language! A foreigner who addresses me in Chinese will have a hard time making himself understood. I do not speak that language. If God were to address me in heavenly phrases or even in the thunder and the lightning, I would not comprehend. Let him, therefore, talk in a language that I can understand, a human language. This he does! Jesus Christ is God getting down to where I live, talking and behaving where I, in my human and limited way, can understand. He is the Word (John 1:1-14) made human.

I once read of a man meditating in the woods who accidentally disturbed a couple of busy ants. They hastily fled in fear. "I'm not going to hurt you, little ants," the man murmured. But the ants paid no attention. They did not speak English. Speculating idly, he realized that if he really were to quiet their fears he would have to become an ant without ceasing to be the human being whose motives and intentions needed interpretation. He would have to lay hold of ant-ness with one hand and of human being-ness with the other, if he were to interpret the higher life to the lower. Then suddenly he realized that this was God's di-lemma, too, and that he solved it in Jesus Christ. The face of the living God was turned toward humanity, and lo, "it was the face of a suffering and rejoicing man."

But we must go deeper. If God be love, then he must do more than appear in our midst with a kind and sympathetic face. To love is to do. If Jesus Christ was to reveal the love of God, he had to do the work of God. He had to involve himself in our sufferings and pain and woe. He had to help, and the help had to be effective.

This brings us to one of the great words of the Christian vocabulary—gospel. The gospel is some kind of good news, and the kind of good news that it claims to be is not duplicated in any other religion. The gospel is the story of what God did in Jesus Christ for humanity's help. And he did it right here in the middle of things, as part (and the most exciting part, at that) of our human story.

The gospel is simply the Christ-story. Thus we speak of the Gospel (i.e., the Christ-story) according to Matthew, the Gospel according to Mark, and so on. The whole sweep of the life and ministry of Christ is involved in the word *gospel*. But its heart is neither in the life nor in the teachings of our Lord. Its center, rather, is in that climactic event which takes up such a proportionately large part of the gospel story—Christ's sacrificial death and triumphant resurrection.

We must be very clear here and careful that we do not go astray. To glorify the death and resurrection of Christ at the expense of his life and teachings would be wrong. His death gains significance from what he was, what he did, and what he said. One should never minimize the great value of the truth which Christ taught. Nor can one ever be too grateful for the perfection of Christ's life. Jesus Christ showed us what a human life really should be. He has become the norm for all others, the standard by which all other lives are judged and evaluated.

But a perfect example and the matchless teachings that go with it are not enough. They do not meet our deepest need. The world does not perish for lack of good advice. We all know more than we put in practice. Our biggest problem is not lack of interest, but lack of ability for doing it. We are like seriously ill patients in a hospital. It is not enough to give such patients instruction in the laws that govern a strong and healthy life. They are too sick for beginning at that point. They may hear and understand, but they cannot do. And appearing before them as a perfect specimen of healthy manhood would only add to their misery. The ways of a well person are not for them. They must be cured of their radical sickness first.

At its heart, then, the gospel is neither the teachings of truth nor their exemplification in life. It is something more. And that "more" is what God has done through Jesus Christ to attack sin at its center and free us of it. And it took a death and a resurrection to do this. "Moreover, brethren, I declare unto you the gospel . . . how that Christ died for our sins . . . And that he was buried, and that he rose again" (1 Cor. 15:1-4). In this redemptive event, the scarred hands of divine love are laid upon our human crookedness and we are made straight. Through this event, the powers of the world to come are let loose to do their healing, changing work. The saving arm of God is here laid bare and the power of the Almighty focused at the point of human need. In short, Jesus Christ is more than a teacher and more than an example. He is a savior. And what is a savior? A savior is someone who does for us what we could not do for ourselves.

As a boy of nine and unable to swim, I almost drowned. My brother, lolling on the bank, could have shouted instructions for a well-executed crawl stroke, but he would have been wasting his breath. I was drowning! Or he could have leaped into the water and bid me follow him. But that, too, would have been futile. I was drowning! My need was for someone to do for me what I could not do for myself. Seeing that I was beyond the help of either information or example, my brother jumped into the water to meet my real need. He saved me.

Salvation! It sounds good, but what is it? Well, it's not just going to heaven when you die. Too long have we been plagued with this narrow interpretation of God's saving mercies. Heaven is part of it—but only part. And even heaven becomes a reality only because of something else that happens first—something that happens right here and now. When the New Testament speaks of salvation, it means "wholeness," nothing less. To be saved is to be made whole; and the same Greek word is sometimes translated as *saved* and sometimes as *made whole*. The theme of the New Testament is how Jesus Christ let loose into society revolutionary forces that attack the radical sickness from which humanity suffers. Through his death and resurrection, a fountain for healing was opened and all who will may drink. To be saved is to be made normal; it means to be healed.[1]

We can now see why it is necessary to be realistic about the seriousness of the sin that afflicts us. If we think that our evil is like a bad cold which we shall shortly throw off, then all that is needed is a determined effort of the will, with a shove or two from God, and all will be well. But if we recognize that our sickness is fatal, then we shall know that self-healing is impossible.

We cannot cure ourselves. We are clever—but not that clever. Only God can arrest the fatal progress of the disease. And it cost God plenty to do the job. The story of the gospel is the story of how God set about to destroy the evil that infects human nature and to restore the soul of man to life and health.

Note

1. Much mischief has been done to new Christians, especially young ones, by giving them the impression that they could expect instant perfection from Christ. When

they discover that they are somewhat less than ideal, their reaction often takes one of two forms, denial or despair. If despair grips them, they usually turn their backs on the Christian faith, deciding it is not for them; they can't live up to it. I remember talking to one such teenager. Finding herself unable to immediately resolve a problem in her relation to her father, she "threw in the towel" remarking to me, "I decided I wasn't good enough for him [God]."

Denial takes a different route. Finding attitudes and feelings which are obviously unchristian cropping up after conversion, the new believer simply looks away, denying their existence, and quietly buries the recognition of such things in the cellar of the unconscious.

What the church should teach is that salvation is not only a present reality but also an ongoing process. The new babe in Christ is just that—a babe. No newborn baby becomes an adult in the twinkling of an eye. Infancy gives way to childhood, childhood to adolescence, adolescence to adulthood. All life is a growth process, including the Christian life.

4
Redemption
from
Guilt

In relation to God, sin means guilt. Guilt spells out a lost fellowship with God. Instead of being Father, God then stands as Judge. Instead of being the trusted One, he becomes the suspected One. Instead of being the One to be sought, he becomes the One to be avoided.

All sin is against God. This is the difference between sin and crime. A crime is perpetrated against a fellow citizen in violation of a law, but sin can only be understood in relation to God. Jesus said, "Thou shalt love the Lord thy God with all thy heart, . . . soul, . . . mind, . . . and . . . strength." Then he said, "This is the first commandment" (Mark 12:30). Defining our main responsibility that way clarifies what constitutes us as sinners. When people say the greatest sin is murder or some other violation of human relations, they only show their ignorance. If the first and greatest commandment is to love God wholly, then the first and greatest sin is not to love God.

To say that people are sinners, then, is to say that they are guilty before God. However much they may try, they cannot avoid some slight suspicion of this truth. Walter Horton once said: "Superficially, 'modern man is not worrying about his sins,' but he is certainly worried about something—worried nearly to death! And an analysis of his behavior shows him trying so feverishly to avoid looking God in the eye that one is surely justified in suspecting that his worries have something to do with the fear of how he would look in God's sight if he should allow himself for a moment to see himself standing in that position."[1]

If we need psychological authority to buttress this truth, we might appeal to Sigmund Freud, who could scarcely be called prejudiced in the matter. Freud insisted that the trace of a feeling of guilt is found in everyone.

If humanity is guilty, the first step in any redemption from sin would have to be forgiveness. That is why the Christian gospel always has had a lot to say about forgiveness. Some people would solve this problem by dismissing it. Thus George Bernard Shaw once said that forgiveness was a word for beggars and that an honest man should pay for his debts. Other people, while believing in forgiveness, approach the problem much too flippantly. They say, "God will forgive; it's his business to forgive." And so saying, they shrug their shoulders and return to their sins. What a pleasant solution for sin! That is to say, God is never so happy as when he is lovingly pardoning my sins. On the other hand, of course, I am never so happy as when I am sinning. So everybody is happy—I in my sinning and God in his forgiving. It is all so easy and satisfying. God will pardon because that is his job. I have nothing to worry about at all.

That is forgiveness—by definition. No wonder people have easy consciences!

Other people say: "I don't think it is as easy as that. But at the same time I don't see why we must identify forgiveness with the horror of a cross and with the pain of the tortured man who hung upon it. All that is necessary for forgiveness is repentance. Let a person repent, and God will forgive."

This theory is plausible and is not wholly lacking in truth. But it must not go unchallenged, for it is far from the whole truth. It leaves untouched the desperate dilemma of God.

Let us assume that God wants to forgive. But how can he? How can God pardon without ruining the character of the pardoned one by a too-cheap forgiveness? Mothers and fathers know what happens if a child gets the impression that forgiveness is simple—a mere matter of saying "I'm sorry" and receiving in return a pat on the head. If doing wrong is so cheaply forgiven, all the seriousness is removed from it. Wrongdoing cannot be so awfully bad because it is so easily pardoned.

Parents who indulge in easygoing and cheap forgiveness encourage children to trade on the parents' good nature and to develop undisciplined character. The son of a Midwestern professor ended up behind prison bars—damned by the tolerance of his sentimental father.

Here, then, is God's problem—how can God forgive without ruining the character of people who take advantage of his good nature by continuing to sin?

This problem is the divine dilemma, and its answer is the cross. The cross declares that pardon is not cheap and easy. On the contrary, it is painful and terribly costly, though it may be offered to the sinner freely. This forgiveness is the wonderful gift of divine love. It was hammered out of the heartbreak and anguish of God himself. The One who forgives is the One who suffers, who offers us pardon at the price of his pain. He lures the guilt of people to his own heart and lets that guilt break it. He bares his own bosom to the dark tides of human sin and lets them engulf it. He draws into the whiteness of his purity the blackness of our evil. And when from the cross comes the divine voice, saying, "I forgive," there is a tragic note in it that reflects the wounds endured on our behalf.

Removal of guilt is here neither inferred from God's nature nor assumed. How could it be? Such an inference or such an assumption could only be human guesswork. Rather the removal of guilt is proclaimed—and it is proclaimed as having been brought to us by the death-marked Christ. The gap between God and humanity had been bridged by God becoming a man and suffering with us and for us and at our hands. "God was in Christ, reconciling the world unto himself" (2 Cor. 5:19). The barrier that guilt had erected between holy God and sinful humanity came crashing down, thrown down from God's side. The restoration of a lost friendship is now possible.

Such a forgiveness is not cheap, nor does it permit one a life of easy sinning. When one sees what sin has cost God, one can never go out and indulge in it lightly again. There is no possibility of taking advantage of God's goodness. There is a price attached to forgiveness; nothing less than the lifeblood of the Son of God could suffice.

Forgiveness is part of the redemption which God has wrought in Christ. But it is only one aspect of the total.

When I was a small boy, my mother purchased a fancy white linen suit for me. She would frequently dress me in it when we went visiting together. But, through intent or accident, rarely was I able to keep clean while waiting for her to finish her own dressing. Five minutes downstairs or in the yard and I was well on the way to becoming filthy. At such times she would interrupt her own preparations, march me off to the bathroom, clean me up, and then announce in her most obedience-inspiring voice: "Now I don't want you to get dirty again. Do you understand, young man?" And I always did!

God, too, is not interested in a forgiveness which leaves us still bent on returning over and over again to the dirt of which we have been pardoned. God says, "Go and sin no more." Salvation is forgiveness—and more.

Note

1. Walter M. Horton, *The Challenge of Our Culture,* ed. Clarence Tucker Craig, chapter 5. Copyright 1946 by Harper & Brothers. Used by permission.

5
Redemption from Perversion

In relation to self, sin means perversion. A few years ago I was visiting a home in the Midwest. The time arrived, as it must to every visitor, when the duty of entertaining the youngster of the family fell upon me. My little blond friend brought me a storybook and soon we were lost in a story. It was a sad story, although it had a happy ending. The hero was a little locomotive which decided it was tired of confining its travels to two rigid rails. To the right and to the left of its roadbed were meadows and brooks and forests. Why would any normal, healthy, young engine ignore all these possibilities in order to stay on the restraining track?

Why, indeed! Soon our little hero of a locomotive had abandoned the rails and had struck out for himself. But so much trouble followed that even a storyteller could scarcely list it all. Unadapted to travel on such terrain, the little engine bumped into trees, careened against stumps, floundered in the mud, and became hopelessly lost. After many horrifying experiences, it managed to extricate itself from the mud and dirt and to get back to the rails again, where it could really make progress.

My little listener was charmed with the story, and so was I, for one of the most puzzling problems of all human experience was raised in that little storybook. One would think that when an engine is free of the rails, it would really have liberty. But such is far from the case. Freed from the rails, the wheels of the engine sink into the mud, and its bulk becomes entangled in the trees and the underbrush. How can it be liberated from these troubles? By finding again the freedom of the rails. But the freedom of the rails was what the locomotive freed itself from in the beginning! The story seems to be a problem of freedom *vs.* freedom. *Freedom* is a very puzzling term.

The experience of the locomotive makes a parable of life. Everyone is confronted with the problem of freedom. If the solution of the problem is wrong, life will be nothing but tragedy and despair. There is freedom—and freedom! One is true freedom and one is false.

The trouble with the little engine in our story was that it had a desire to be free of its own limitations. It was made to function only upon rails, but that did not satisfy it. It aspired to an independence and a self-sufficiency which would not tie it to its created destiny. In other words, it was a sinner in the full biblical sense of the term. Man's problem grows out of this same kind of false independence. We are sinners because we are not satisfied to be what God wants us to be. We feel constrained and hemmed in by the demands of God, so we throw them aside and strike out for ourselves. We want to be independent, to manage our own lives, to do what we want to do when we want to do it.

But our liberty turns out to be illusory. Like the locomotive, we get stuck in the mud. Only the mud, in this case, is sin.

The false freedom of independence from God leads to the bondage of sin. This is the constant witness of the New Testament. Seeming freedom is really slavery. This is the truth about sinners. We are slaves.

Sometimes our bondage is to certain pleasures. Sometimes we become enslaved to various appetites. At other times our greatest tyranny is the opinion of others. Perhaps we may let this latter kind of bondage illustrate the strange way by which freedom leads to slavery. Take a look at the average person in the street who takes pride in personal liberty. Notice the clothes. Don't they look like the clothes everyone else is wearing? Of course they do. This person comes home from work and turns on the television to the same show the neighbors are watching. The tune she whistles is probably either a catchy commercial jingle or a recent popular song. She smokes the same cigarettes, drinks the same liquor, tells the same jokes, goes to the same places, and does the same things everybody else does. When talking, she gives utterance to the same prejudices and opinions that millions of other people have.

Advertisers tell a person what to buy; radio, television and newspapers tell him what to believe. In short, he is a pretty pathetic figure, a cross between a person and a mouse. He spends his life in fear of being different, in bondage to conformity, in slavery to the opinion of the group to which he belongs. Almost every breath is dictated by habit or social pressure. He is a regimented little sheep—just one of the flock. But he will not touch God with a ten-foot pole because he wants to be free— master of his fate, captain of his soul.[1]

But if there is a liberty of death, a liberty of bondage, there is also a liberty of life. If there is a false freedom, there is also a true freedom. Real liberty is the liberty of a locomotive rolling freely along its rails to the destination it has in view. Real liberty is the liberty of proper functioning. It is the liberty of the tree, planted by the rivers of water, that grows and realizes itself according to its kind. True freedom is the liberty of people who realize themselves according to the laws of being, who fulfill themselves according to the way they were made.

Sin has created this problem of bondage in the false liberty of independence from God. In our folly, we've become all "gummed up." And just as we saw that only God could remove our guilt by an act of forgiveness, so only God can correct our perversion by an act of deliverance. Perversion means inability and incapacity—inability to do what we ought, to live as we ought, to be what we ought. This is why—a great puzzle to many—the Christian faith does not *begin* with appeals for right living or start with the Golden Rule and the Sermon on the Mount. It *ends* with them, but begins with something entirely different—a story, the story of Jesus and his love. And the puzzled visitor shakes his head as he leaves the church muttering to himself, "The world is going to hell and these people are still living 1900 years ago." But he's wrong. If a person is in a wheelchair, paralyzed from the waist down, you do not mock such misery by giving instructions in the art of walking. You first restore the use of the legs and *then* teach the person to walk. If a person is blind, you do not begin with the rules for detection of color difference. You take away the blindness. If a person is in shackles, you do not give a map for a journey. You set him loose.

The Christian faith sees humanity in the full dimensions of perversion. The twist in a heart cannot be cured by wishing things were otherwise; much less by ignoring it as if it were not there. The wholeness that means liberty of growth and development can come only from a major operation. Deliverance is a divine gift. Only God can make the crooked straight and the perverted whole.

God does it in that mighty act of divine redemption which he wrought in Jesus Christ. Humanity lay under the dominion of alien powers. Sin and death held sway. Then came the White Knight of heaven to grapple with the powers of darkness. All hell moved up to defeat the Challenger. At the cross there was a head-on collision between love and hate, life and death, heaven and hell. Sin did its worst—and it was not enough. Death did its worst—and its victory was short lived. "He broke the power of sin and death and set the captive free." The Son of God hurled himself at the juggernaut of the world's evil; though it crushed him, he broke it. Sin and death had met their master; and all who sought the help of the divine Deliverer could share his victory. In his presence the tyrannies of life fell away and people could stand erect. "The liberty of the sons of God" had become an actuality.

Nygren, the famous Swedish theologian, has told a modern story to illustrate the nature of the deliverance which Christ effected. For five long years during World War II, Denmark had lain under the brutal oppression of the invader. Then in the spring of 1945 the Nazis, hammered relentlessly all over Europe by the Allies, suddenly withdrew to the borders of Germany. Out from the big cities to the places where brave patriots hid in terror of their lives went a message. What was it? "Be courageous"? "Be kind"? "Do your best"? Oh, no! The message was a simple recital of something that had happened: "The invader has been defeated. Denmark is free!" And brave people breathed again the air of liberty, and fugitives returned to their homes and businesses and walked again along the streets and lanes of an emancipated Denmark.

The gospel of Jesus Christ is a message like that. It is not an appeal to the highest ideals, although that is important and involved

in the total Christian structure. It is not a proc-
lamation of general religious truths—the existence of God, his holiness and love, the
immortality of the soul, and similar ideas
(although these too are important in their
place). It is the telling of a story, of something
that happened in a particular time and place. It
is the message of how, in Jesus Christ, God
decisively intervened in the tragedy of our
human history and effected a great deliverance
in which all may share who listen believingly to
the message.

Note

1. The humorist Art Buchwald tells of a group of young
people in Berkeley, California, when Berkeley was so
much in the public eye. Buchwald mentions how they
were all wearing beards, long hair, sandals, beads, and
similarity of clothing. Each was carrying a placard with
the same message: "Be different." Wonderfully true to
life even if Buchwald made it up.

6
Redemption from Lovelessness

In relation to others, sin means unbrotherliness, lovelessness.

What happens when a person is converted? Well, several things may happen. He gets a new set of beliefs, a new moral direction, and probably a new emotional tone to life. While all of these things are involved and all are important, none of them represents the center of the experience. In a true conversion, where the living God is really met, "the love of God is shed abroad in our hearts by the Holy Ghost" (Rom. 5:5). Christian conversion is a rebirth into a love that is not our own, but God's.

We had better take a long look at this word *love*. The Greek language has several words for love, but English is poor at this point. Indeed, one hesitates to use the word at all because its meaning has been so totally usurped by one form of love, the romantic kind.

We are familiar with two basic kinds of love: *craving* love and *giving* love. Craving love represents the thrill that comes once in a lifetime. It is that yearning desire to be loved, to be wanted, to belong. It may be an exceedingly selfish thing. The boy may sing into the ear of the girl, "I love you, I love you, I love you," when really he means, "I love me and want you." The divorce rate in this country is abnormally high because too many people "fall in love" only for what they hope to get out of the relationship.

Opposed to craving love is giving love. This love is the kind which seeks to offer itself for the good of another and to live its life in the life of the beloved. This love is the only kind upon which a stable marriage can be built.

Craving love and giving love—this is one possible division of love. Is there another way in which we can analyze love? Can we speak of human love and divine love and really mean something important by this distinction? If we can, then craving love and giving love would be subdivisions of the human kind, and love of a divine kind would be something different in quality, though not unrelated.

We had better move very carefully here because, if we misunderstand the Christian faith at this point, we are going to make our whole discussion fatally defective. Let us begin with the way in which Jesus summarized the Law and the Prophets: "Thou shalt love the Lord thy God with all thy heart, and with all thy soul, and with all thy mind. This is the first and great commandment. And the second is like unto it, Thou shalt love thy neighbour as thyself'' (Matt. 22:37-39). Now, it has generally been recognized by nominal Christians, that we should love our neighbors. But why did Christ make love of neighbor second and insist that love of God be first? The answer has important implications. Jesus was telling us that we cannot love our neighbors unless we first loved God—at least we cannot love neighbors in the way we are supposed to love. The kind of love which the New Testament insists upon can only be enduring and secured against self-regarding tendencies if it is derived from a love of God.

Was Jesus right or wrong when he said this? ''Wrong,'' cries the world. ''There are people who love their neighbors—fine, upright, idealistic, kindly people—who can't make up their minds whether God even exists. They love without benefit of clergy or religion.'' So says the world, and apparently many are in agreement with this general position. Many years ago, a national magazine made a survey. In this survey, they asked people what they thought the world needed more than anything else. The answer of eight out of ten queried was, ''More love for each other, the way Jesus said." The next question that was asked was, "Do you think that you love your neighbor the way Jesus said we should?" And eight out of ten of them said, "Yes."

This is pretty serious and shows how tragically the modern world has misunderstood the Christian faith. Most people assume that what we owe our neighbors is kindness or goodwill or some similar human virtue which can be expressed as occasions arise. But if all that is meant by Christian love is the virtue of what the world calls kindness, why all the talk about God and a cross and a new birth? You really do not have to know God or to be a Christian in order to develop a personality which can reveal gracious goodwill toward others. But what if Christian love is more than such kind ness? What if the kindness which is demanded of us is so high, so godlike, that no human being could hope to attain it? What if Christian love is a quality of life which is so superhuman that it brings us to despair just to think about the demands it makes upon us? In short, what if God asks of us what we cannot give him? What is left for us to respond except, "Woe is me! for I am a man of unclean lips, and I dwell in the midst of a people of unclean lips"? (Isa. 6:5).

We are now about to step upon holy ground. The world is dying for lack of a radical, reckless, self-renouncing love for others. But this kind of radical love that is demanded is not an ethical principle nor a human virtue which we can attain if we work at it hard enough. This kind of love is *agape*-love, to use the untranslatable Greek name for it. It is of the very nature and heart of the eternal God. This radical, superhuman love developed human form and came to us in Jesus Christ. The love nature of God is spelled out in the life and ministry of our Lord Jesus Christ, the One who sacrificed himself even for his enemies.

What follows? That we should imitate Jesus and love as he did? To say this is to lose the point, for it makes of love a mere human virtue which is within our power to achieve. It is our despair that we cannot love as God would have us love. This is precisely what it means to be radically flawed. And it is at this juncture that the death of Christ upon the cross comes again into view. Through the offering of himself in death, the love of God has found a channel to the human heart. Through his resurrection, the heart of God, which is love, becomes available as the content of the life of every human being who seeks it.

The love of God becomes poured into receptive and open hearts through the Holy Spirit. This is the *new birth* which the living Christ effects. We are made new in and for love—the divine, not a merely human, love. Our sinful selves find their Master, and we become channels of a new quality of life—the supernatural love of God, both incarnated and made available in Jesus Christ. This is no human possession! It is a divine gift acquired only by faith and surrender. That is why we can have a dependable neighbor-love only if we have first come to grips with God. For we love with the love wherewith we were loved. We love with a love which is not our own, for in very truth it is God who loves through us. We are channels of his grace and mercy.

"Owe no man any thing, but to love one another" (Rom. 13:8), said Paul. And if we did, in a Christian sense, what a revolutionary effect it would have upon both the church and the world! The whole field of responsible social action comes into view at this point. The tensions in our social order—racial, economic, political, international—await the ministry of the sons of Love. Only love can make us concerned, and only love can produce results in changed social relations and perspectives. It is a solemn responsibility to assume the name Christian. Many lightly pin on the label who do not possess the life. Where there is no concern, there is no Christianity!

7
Redemption
to
Goodness

Be good," we airily say, as we murmur pleasant good-byes. And thereby we repeat an illusion under which the world has long lived: It is not too hard to be good! True, it is not a very pleasant experience; you will have more fun if you "weaken just a little." But if a man really sets his mind to it, he can follow the Golden Rule and cultivate various virtues and make of himself a good man.

If this were true, no Christian gospel would be necessary. If it were true, Jesus was a very misleading teacher. A young man once came running to Jesus, and, prostrating himself at his feet, addressed him in these words: "Good Master, what shall I do that I may inherit eternal life?"

But Jesus interrupted him. "Why callest thou me good?" he said. "There is none good but one, that is God" (Mark 10:17-18). The young man had been perfectly sincere in his salutation. He had seen in Jesus a real and appealing goodness, and his heart had responded accordingly. But Jesus repudiated the term for all humanity! There is nobody good but the eternal and holy God.

Suppose that you paid a bill and received five dollars as change. On Sunday you go to church and, placing the five-dollar bill in an envelope, you put it on the offering plate. The bill helps the church pay the minister's salary. The minister buys groceries with it; the grocery man in turn uses it to help pay his rent; it helps the landlord in turn to buy a suit; and with it the tailor buys milk for his children. Thus the five-dollar bill circulates through society, doing much good in the process, until it finally arrives at the bank. There an inspector takes one look at it, hesitates, takes another close look, and marks it for destruction. Your poor little five-dollar bill was counterfeit! It went about the world doing good, but when it arrived at the place where real values count, it just could not get by. It *did* good, but it *wasn't* good.

The distinction between goodness as conduct and goodness as a quality of life was exactly the point that Jesus was trying to make with the rich young ruler. You can do good without too much difficulty. For that, you do not need to have a saving experience of the grace of God. You do not even need to believe that there is a God in order to achieve good conduct. But to *be* good—that is something entirely different. The quality of life called goodness is not a human quality at all. Men may do good but only God *is* good.

This, of course, confronts everyone with a problem that is little short of desperate. I know that goodness is expected of me. It is laid upon me as a demand which I cannot evade. But in the same breath, I am assured that I cannot meet the demand. If goodness is an attribute of God and not of humanity, I am licked before I start. Or am I? Well, there would seem to be one way out. If the goodness which is God could somehow get into me, then I, too, could really be good. This divine goodness is exactly what the gospel offers to me. Second Peter, extolling the power and mercy of Christ, exclaims: "Whereby are given unto us exceeding great and precious promises: that by these ye might be partakers of the divine nature" (1-4). "Partakers of the divine nature"! This, of course, would solve our problem. The goodness which is God would come pouring into our souls and recreate us in its own likeness.

The goodness which is God, like the love which is God, is both seen and made available in Jesus Christ; and these two are one. As with love, so with goodness. We cannot look at the divine goodness in Christ and then say, I will follow Christ and imitate this. Such an easy solution to the problem, as we have seen all along, overlooks the seriousness of our sin. But through the sacrifice of Christ on the cross, this goodness is made available to us as a divine gift. We follow Christ only because first we have found him as the guest of our soul, and his goodness lives itself out anew in us.

It remains to point out only one thing more. It is because the Christian faith makes of goodness a divine gift rather than a human achievement that it can solve the problem of self-righteousness. Nietzsche said, "The good must be Pharisees—they have no choice." And he was right if morality is a human achievement. If I have attained to goodness by my own efforts, I would have every right to be proud of myself. But if I am proud, I am not humble. And if I am not humble, I really am not good at all! I am merely self-righteous. This is the paradox of all humanistic ethics.

Only the Christian faith can save a good man from the accusation which Nietzsche leveled. Only God is good—and those to whom God imparts himself. The gift excludes all boasting.

8
The
Conquering
Christ

It may seem that a man has a great deal of nerve to attempt the writing of a few brief chapters setting forth in nine easy lessons the fundamentals of the Christian faith. There are a lot of fundamentals connected with the Christian faith, and many of them I have not touched on at all. All that I have tried to do is to illumine the meaning of the Christian gospel. If we understand what the gospel is, we are at the heart of what God wants us to know. We can be pretty hazy about some things in the Christian faith, but what is absolutely essential is our understanding of the meaning and mission of Jesus Christ.

We have seen that the gospel is the story of God's wondrous acts in Jesus Christ. Sin has undone us, but God was not satisfied to leave us to sin. Sin has disturbed our relationships to God, to ourselves, and to other human beings. Christ has done for us what we could not do for ourselves. He has restored our fellowship with God through removing our guilt; this is forgiveness. He has restored us to our true selves by saving us from our worst selves; this is freedom. He has set right our upset relationships with other humans by binding us to each other in love. Through these changes, which are all part of the same change, we have become good—good in a goodness which is not our own, but which belongs to another.

All this transformation God has effected through the crucifixion-resurrection of Jesus Christ. We should not separate the crucifixion from the resurrection. We tend to talk much about the cross and to make mention of the resurrection only at Easter. But when we do so, we are separating something that cannot rightly be separated. To see the cross in isolation, without the light of Easter shining upon it, is not to see the Christian cross at all, but only a mere instrument of torture, a mere stick of wood. Now, after this acknowledgment that the crucifixion and the resurrection ought not be separated, for brevity's sake I am going to separate them and talk about what the resurrection of Christ means in the Christian scheme of things.

The resurrection is the key that unlocks the mysteries of the Bible. The teachings and ministry of Jesus Christ did not give the early disciples a gospel. Our Lord, on the contrary, left his disciples deeply puzzled, almost in panic. Only after the resurrection did everything make sense. That is why the preaching of the early church stressed the resurrection of Jesus Christ beyond all other themes. The resurrection gave the world a new book, a new day, and a new institution. The new book is, of course, the New Testament, of which God is the hero. It is only by virtue of the resurrection that the Bible is a unit and that its message is coherent and true. The new day is Sunday, the Lord's Day, set aside for commemorating Jesus' emergence from the tomb. The new institution is the Christian church, which never would have come into being without Easter.

Some have said that the lesson which we should learn from Easter is that the soul is immortal. But this is not at all what the early disciples learned from it. They did not preach survival, but resurrection. In their minds, the two were related, but very different. Survival means that something called the soul keeps right on living after death. This belief is not peculiar to Christianity; and the preaching of survival would not have been a revolutionary teaching, for many great teachers before the Christian era had taught it. What the early disciples preached was that someone who was dead had risen from the dead. This was resurrection; the tomb was empty. And by the time they had grasped this fact and had related it to the cross and, indeed, to the whole history of the Hebrew people, they were ready to preach something that the world had never heard before. The God who raised Jesus Christ from the dead had begun a new chapter in human history. The resurrection of Jesus Christ meant that a unique, redemptive, and creative intervention of God into human affairs had taken place. A new day had dawned.

What did the resurrection mean to the early Christians? For one thing, it meant the vindication of Jesus Christ and the assurance of his final triumph. Some of the most crucial questions about the nature of the universe were raised in their ultimate form by the death of Jesus Christ. These questions had haunted men for centuries as they had tried to grope their way to some understanding of what life was all about. They had asked themselves, for example: Why is there so much suffering and pain in the universe if there is a God? Why does hate seem so strong and love so weak? Why do good people suffer and wicked people prosper?

Never in the history of the world were these questions raised more pointedly than in the death of Jesus Christ. The best man who ever lived had tried to serve his Heavenly Father, and he had ended up nailed to a cross. How can there be a good God if such things happen?

It is easy to look at the cross of Christ and let it turn you into an atheist. It threatened to do that to the early disciples—and then God answered their questionings and doubts by a resurrection. The resurrection was God's signature of approval upon the ministry and teachings of Jesus Christ. By raising Jesus from the dead, God showed that the universe backs goodness and not badness. As E. Stanley Jones put it, evil can go a long, long way. It can even crucify the Son of God. It can win the first day and it can win the second day. But the third day—no. On the third day God speaks. And what he said on that third day in the long ago was a message that every generation needs to hear. Love is stronger than hate, justice is mightier than injustice, truth is more powerful than falsehood, God is stronger than the devil.

The resurrection may be likened to the recognition scene in a great drama. Most of the epics of world literature have as their climax a revelatory scene in which what was hidden becomes disclosed. Detective stories end in a final burst of discovery in which the preceding episodes fall into place and make sense. The last act gives the clue to all that went before. Canon Wedel suggests that the resurrection of Jesus was just such a climactic and revealing event, and he compares it with the act of self-disclosure that climaxes Homer's famous story, the *Odyssey*. "Odysseus returns home in beggar's disguise—a king's incognito. He is 'despised and rejected of men,' an outcast in his own palace. At last, in the climactic scene, when Odysseus alone can stretch the royal bow and win the archery contest, the 'beggar' is revealed as the 'king.' "[1] So Christ. He came unto his own disguised as a poor peasant. He was reviled and crucified. But at the resurrection the bewildered disciples saw the parts of the puzzle fall into place. These events through which they had passed were not as they had seemed. God had been in their midst, working out his mighty acts of redemption. This friendless and unresisting man whom wicked men had killed was in reality the Lord of history, the Christ of God. The beggar was, in reality, the King of kings and Lord of lords.

But it was only his friends who recognized him through the resurrection. The eyes of the world were still blind to what was going on. The last that the world at large saw of the great Lover was his defeat at the cross. The forces of evil thought they had rid themselves of him and had overthrown his cause, but they were deceived. The victory that Christ won by rising triumphant over sin and the grave will some day be obvious to all. The forces of evil have received their death warrant, though they still have the power to inflict much suffering. In the warfare of God against evil, the resurrection of Christ was the turning point. Through the resurrection, the Christian sees that Christ has already broken the power of evil in the world and has let loose into it the healing forces of the world to come. The love which was rejected of men and crucified, which the Christian sees even now as risen and triumphant, will one day rule the world. The resurrection of Christ is a pledge of the final victory of the kingdom of God.

This is what the New Testament means when it talks about the return of Christ. Today, Christ is head of a government-in-exile; however, he left an active underground in enemy territory (the Christian movement). When the final scene of the Christian drama takes place, the crucified one will be revealed as the victorious Captain of the hosts of heaven, and every tongue will declare him Lord to the glory of God. A straight line runs from his rejection at the cross, through the resurrection, to his final and complete victory.

Meanwhile the resurrection of Jesus

Christ means that he is alive and available. As William Temple, the former archbishop of Canterbury, used to say, it is not enough to say that Jesus Christ is alive. All who have died are alive, but nonetheless they are lost to their loved ones on earth. William Temple sought to remind us that Christ is both alive *and available.* Through his "other self," the Holy Spirit, his presence is still with us. He can be talked to and can, in return, guide and help those who are his followers.

When Jesus Christ was here in the body, he was limited to being in one place at a given time. If he were in Jerusalem, he could not be in Capernaum. But his resurrection means that he is no longer limited. Through prayer, he is available to everyone who needs his help. Having himself lived a life of total obedience, even unto death, to the will of his Heavenly Father, he now, as the risen Lord, turns around to his disciples and says, "I'll show you how I did it." He gives not only guidance but powerful ability too.

The resurrection of Christ indicates to us our own destiny. Because he lives, we too shall live. His resurrection is the pledge of our own resurrection. This has often been interpreted to mean that we can all be sure of the immortality of our souls. But the New Testament conceives it in a slightly different way. The New Testament teaches that the salvation of God extends to the whole person, including his body. However, this does not mean a merely physical resurrection of bodies-as-they-now-are, for we read that flesh and blood cannot inherit the kingdom of God. Rather, the body principle is transformed into a spiritual body, which is a perfect vehicle of the spirit. But the point is that all of a person shares in God's redemption.

The resurrection of the body is what distinguishes the Hebrew way of thinking from the Greek way of thinking. To some Greeks, body and matter were evil and had to be cast aside before the soul could be freed for its destiny. But in biblical thought, matter and the body are not evil at all, as long as they perform their proper functions as the vehicle through which the spirit expresses itself. The Hebrews took life, history, and the temporal seriously. That is why Reinhold Niebuhr said that no article in the Apostles' Creed expresses the genius of Christianity more neatly than the words "I believe in the resurrection of the body."

Finally, through the resurrection of Christ

every believer participates in the perfect humanity which was Christ's. The Christian faith expresses this in different ways. Perhaps the most characteristic way of putting it is found in the phrase "union with Christ." To be "in Christ" is to be a partaker of his nature. The risen Lord is the head of a new people which are united to him as the source of life. He is the head, and we are the body; he is the vine, and we are the branches. All that we are or hope to be depends on our union with him. He is the representative man to whom we are organically related.

The togetherness associated with the term "union with Christ" means that we must repeat in our experience, spiritually, something of what Christ went through when he was here on earth. He was crucified. We, too, must die to self. He was raised from the dead. We, too, must rise from the tomb of our sins into newness of life. And the new life into which we rise is no less than his life shared with us. "I am crucified with Christ: nevertheless I live; yet not I, but Christ liveth in me" (Gal. 2:20). And because we share his life, we shall share also his destiny as glorified children of God. In the words of Leslie Weatherhead, a Christian is a friend of Jesus Christ. And this friendship is and remains transforming.

To sum it all up, there are four pillars of the Christian faith. The first is the life of Christ. The second is the death of Christ, and the third is his resurrection. These are a part of what happened two thousand years ago. If it is to be worth anything to us, what happened long ago must get into the individual heart. The fourth pillar of the Christian faith is the moment of inward renewal when, by surrender and commitment to him, the Christ of history becomes the internal Christ. The personality of Jesus then links itself redemptively to the personality of the believer, and these two become one.

Perhaps I can explain best just what the resurrection means practically to the Christian by a little make-believe. It happens that as I write this an appeal for funds for hospitalized veterans lies opened upon my desk. It is signed by one of the great violinists of our time. Suppose someone, noting the skillfulness with which the master musician handled his instrument, said to me: "Now there is your example. You go out and play a violin like that." Such a demand would be my despair. I am just not capable of imitating such virtuosity. Nor will instruction eliminate the gap between the master musician and myself. I am no musical genius. But if by some miracle, he could get inside me and use my body to express his musical soul and technique, then I could play like him. But it would not be I, but the master within me. I could claim no credit; it would be by grace. No honor could accrue to me; I merely had had the sense to yield myself to his sway. I had let him take over.

To ask a person to follow Jesus or to obey his teachings is merely to drive that person to despair. But if Jesus Christ could become the Guest of that person's soul and live life all over again through that body, things would be different. Christian faith insists that Jesus Christ can do just that!

Note

1. Canon Theodore Wedel, *The Christianity of Main Street.* Copyright 1950 by The Macmillan Company. Used by permission.

9
The Price and
the Prize

In Lewis Carroll's *Through the Looking Glass* there is an instructive dialogue between Alice and the White Queen.

QUEEN: How old are you?

ALICE: I'm seven and a half exactly.

QUEEN: You needn't say "exactly." I can believe it without that. Now I'll give *you* something to believe. I'm just one hundred and one, five months, and a day.

ALICE: I can't believe *that*.

QUEEN *(in a pitying tone):* Can't you? Try again. Draw a long breath, and shut your eyes.

ALICE *(laughing):* There is no use trying. One *can't* believe impossible things.

QUEEN: I dare say you haven't had much practice. When I was your age I always did it for half an hour a day. Why, sometimes I've believed as many as six impossible things before breakfast.

There are many people who, knowing nothing about Christianity, have assumed that the Christian faith means taking a deep breath, shutting one's eyes, and believing what one knows deep down inside is absolutely incredible. Faith is, of course, nothing of the sort. But before we indicate just what it is, it may be helpful to remember that any view of the universe, even atheism, is a faith. The facts of life and of the world are accessible to all. But the way in which we arrange these facts in an effort to extract from them their *meaning* is an act of faith.

We always look at our world from the viewpoint of a perspective, a perspective which is chosen in terms of what, to us, seems of crucial significance. One may choose matter, nature, or scientific method as of crucial importance. Another may choose mind or values as crucial. The important thing to remember is that everybody looks at the facts of life from a viewpoint, a perspective. This perspective provides the framework by which each person arranges the facts so that they tell a story, that is, make sense to him. And this standpoint, whatever it may be, is *chosen*. It is an act of faith. So, whether I call myself an atheist or an agnostic or a believer in God, I have a faith! The Christian is no worse off at this point than is his opponent.

Now Christianity anchors itself in Jesus Christ. It chooses him as the supremely important fact of human experience. He provides the perspective from which it views the world. He becomes the clue by which the meaning of life and the world are to be unraveled. "Having faith" means something quite specific and special to Christians. To have faith in the Christian sense is (a) to believe a story and (b) to trust and obey a person.

The story to be believed is the story of the gospel which we have been tracing—that God was in Christ, reconciling the world unto himself. This Christ died for our sins, rose triumphant for our deliverance, and wields the saving power of God.

To believe in the redemptive event which God effected in Christ is necessary, but not sufficient. To stop here would make Christian faith purely *belief that*. This would leave out the factor of *obedience to,* which is absolutely essential. To *believe that* is to assume a set of ideas. And no set of ideas—not even the greatest set of ideas that the mind of man knows, the gospel—can save us. We need to find not the power of ideas, but the power of God— and God is not an idea.

Suppose that you are desperately sick—so sick that only a major operation demanding great skill can save your life. A friend comes to you and says, "I know just the man who is able to meet your need. He is a famous surgeon who lives in such and such a city. His name is William Smith, his address is 818 Jones Street, and his telephone number is 555-7849. He is forty years old, married, and has three children. He is one of the best-known men in his field in the country. Do you believe this?"

And you say, "Yes, I believe."

Whereupon your friend convulsively grasps your hand, squeezes it, and says with emotion: "Thank God. Now you're all healed. You can go back to work in the morning."

You probably would think that the poor man had completely lost his mind. For it is very obvious that no set of facts about a surgeon or a physician would be of any help in a fatal disease. Such ideas could only serve as means to a larger end, and that end would be getting the physician in question to take the case, surrendering yourself to his care, and letting his skill do whatever needs to be done.

In the Christian system, the same thing is true. No set of ideas about Jesus Christ—about who he is, about his nature, about what he can do and what he will do—is enough to redeem us. We must get the Redeemer himself in on our case. We must surrender ourselves to his care and his skill must go to work if we are to be made whole. So if one part of Christian faith is *belief that* something has happened, the other part is *trust in* and *surrender to* the Redeemer of whom the gospel speaks. The story (that is to say, the gospel) points to the Person. A Christian is someone who has a passion for this Person.

Christian faith, then, is that attitude of inward commitment by which a man comes to the end of himself and trusts his life—past, present, and future—to the care and skill of the crucified and risen Christ, that is, the Christ of the story. This trusting surrender is an oath of allegiance. That is why Karl Barth said that faith is standing at attention: "Lord, what wouldest thou have me to do?" To have faith—*Christian* faith—is to acquire a Lord over ones' life. It is decisive choice of Christ, his mercies, and his will.

A story to be believed, a Person to be obeyed: this is the core of the church's preaching. The modern church has much that it would say as it enters into dialogue with a fearful, insecure, and sundered world. But the one redeeming word which is at the heart of its message is the same word which Paul spoke in the long ago to the groping jailer at Philippi: "Believe on the Lord Jesus Christ, and thou shalt be saved" (Acts 16:31). The price of salvation is high to both God and man. To God the price was nails; to man, the death of self. But the cost is high because the stake is high. The prize is LIFE itself.